Congratulations on buying your
around-the-galaxy ticket with Peril Space Tours!

My name is Captain Peril. When touring with us you'll encounter
many strange and possibly dangerous puzzles.
Just follow the instructions in this guide and you probably
won't get eaten or blasted into antimatter.

Good luck, and thank you
for choosing to fly with Peril Space Tours.

DAY ONE
The Ramshackle

Welcome aboard Peril Space Tours' luxury star cruiser "The Ramshackle". This charming relic will be carrying you to some of the most astounding puzzle destinations of the known galaxy—that is, if it doesn't blow up first!

The space-warp generators are overloading! There are four different generator cut-off circuits around the ship, and all but one are broken. Can you find the working circuit and press the button before we are reduced to subatomic particles?

You will be using the automated lander to fly down to a planet's surface.

To activate the lander, press the button that completes the sequence.

DAY TWO
Whitewater rafting on the crystal moon of Eridani

The crystal moon of Eridani is well known for its stunning landscapes and winding acid rivers. What better way is there to experience them than from an inflatable raft?

Make your way through the acid-river maze to the Moon Juice Saloon, and try not to get snagged on the sharp crystals!

To buy a drink at the
Moon Juice Saloon
will cost four
yellow crystals.

Can you find them
along the way?

DAY THREE
Flappadon spotting in the wildlife reserve of Tau Ceti

The wildlife reserve of Tau Ceti is home to the last known family of flappadons, the largest flying creatures in the galaxy. You can watch them from the lookout on Spotter's Peak.

It is said that a flappadon won't try to eat you if you can see it. There are five flappadons in the wildlife reserve. Can you see them all?

DAY FOUR
The Halls of Naught on Planet Nix

Deep in the centre of the Coal Sack Nebulae lies Planet Nix, home to the Halls of Naught.

To enter the Halls of Naught you must pass the dreaded Gates of Null. Touch the screen that equals zero to get in... And be careful!

(6−3)x2

(6x3)−2

6−(3x2)

(3−2)x6

Within the Halls of Naught the Null Masters contain all the Nothing known to exist. They must concentrate on Nothing, to prevent it from engulfing the universe. If something happens it will distract them, and Nothing will escape to happen everywhere!

Can you spot all ten situations where a Null Master could be distracted?

DAY FIVE
Bathe in the glop pools of Draconis V

It's time to slow down and relax in the warm, health-bringing glop pools of Draconis' fifth planet. Starting from ground level, use the ladders to find your way to the only spare glop pool.

To dry off afterwards, you can use one of the spare towels. Don't use towels with blue stripes, as they belong to glopdrakes. Avoid any towels with red spots, as they are yesterday's, and are all dirty.

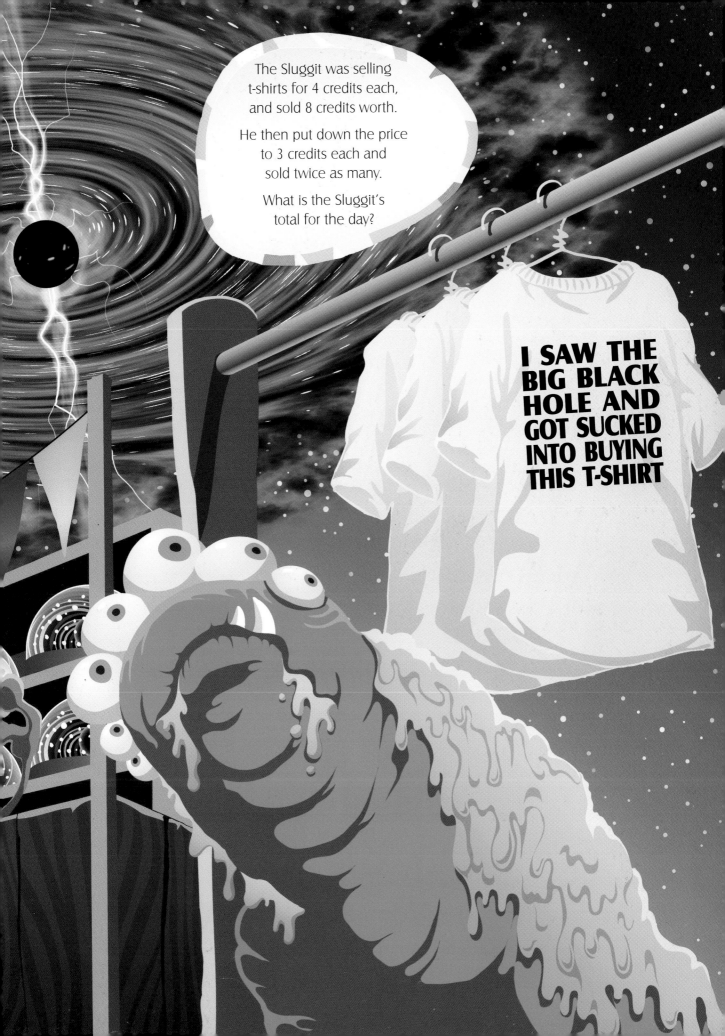

DAY SEVEN
The abandoned ruins of Leporis IV

Long ago the Leporins mysteriously vanished, leaving behind only their buildings and pets. We caught some of these pets in cages, so you could have a closer look. Perhaps you should release them before their mothers get angry.

Can you find the eight keys to unlock each of the cages?

DAY EIGHT
Ranch stay on Alpha Centauri III

It's round-up time in the rolling pink grasslands of Alpha Centauri's third planet, where you'll stay on a ranch and help muster a wuffer herd. First you'll have to find a wuffer trained for riding!

A trained wuffer won't have any pink spots, its tusks will be trimmed and it will have a saddle on its back. Beware—the untrained wuffers always bite!

Wuffers like to be put into their pens in pairs. Can you find the matching pair for each wuffer already in a pen?

DAY NINE
The City of Illusion on Rana II

Don't believe your eyes when in the City of Illusion! The Ranans love visual trickery, so they build their cities to fool the eyes. There are ten differences between the city and its reflection in the lake.

Can you spot all ten?

DAY TEN

Evasive action with the space pirates

The Ramshackle spends a lot of time in the lawless depths of space, so sooner or later we always run into some space pirates.

These fun-loving free booters are currently locking their weapons on to us, but we can stop each ship by working out the secret number that disables their energy system.

Make the rows of numbers on each ship add up to the same amount and you will find its secret number!

Hurry, before they use their disintegration rays on us!

DAY ELEVEN
The Galacto Rock Festival of Vega IV

Turn up, plug in and drop out at the Galacto Rock Festival!

The Lyrans are on stage and want to play their hit song "Holding Tentacles with You", but they have forgotten how to plug their instruments into the amplifiers. Can you help them plug in before the crowd gets angry?

Guess which symbol comes next in each of the patterns on the amplifiers and match the symbols to their instruments.

DAY TWELVE
The Last Resort at Fomalhaut

Tourists come to the famous Last Resort when there's nowhere left to go. It was built inside an asteroid orbiting Fomalhaut, and from the outside looks strangely like a big fish head. Can you spot which asteroid contains the Last Resort? Watch out—as the other asteroids often contain giant space worms.

SPACE WORM
PETTING ZOO
10 credits

FLARE SOLARIUM
10 credits

PARA ROCKETIN
50 credits

Inside the Last Resort there are six wild activities to try. There are also delicious Space Worm Smoothies for your refreshment.

You have exactly 100 galactic credits to spend.

If you are to try every activity and get a smoothie, should you pay for each activity separately, buy one of the multipasses, or use a combination?

100-CREDI
MULTIPAS

Gets you in
all activitie

Smoothie
not includ

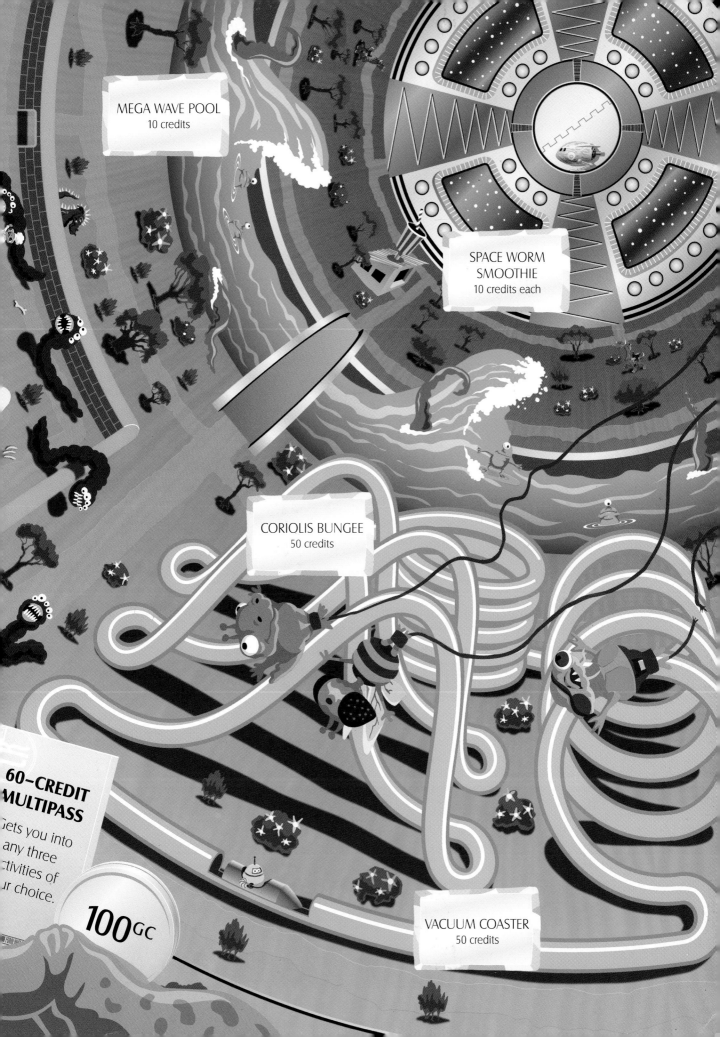

MEGA WAVE POOL
10 credits

SPACE WORM
SMOOTHIE
10 credits each

CORIOLIS BUNGEE
50 credits

**60-CREDIT
MULTIPASS**
Gets you into
any three
activities of
your choice.

100GC

VACUUM COASTER
50 credits

TOO
FAR
BACK!

DAY THIRTEEN
Time warp to Planet Earth

You have survived your Peril Space Tour.
Now it's time to warp back to Earth.
Unfortunately, because we've spent a lot of
time travelling faster than light, 400 years have
passed on Earth! It's a good thing our ship has
its own on-board time machine.

Follow the time channels back
to the Earth you remember.

WAY
TOO
FAR
BACK!

Welcome home intrepid space explorer! We seem to have left your luggage behind somewhere. Perhaps you can go back and search for it...

Your luggage looks like this.

We also seem to have lost our crew. Can you go back and find them too?

The missing crew members look like this.

SOLUTIONS

DAY ONE

DAY TWO

DAY THREE

DAY FOUR

DAY FIVE

DAY SIX

The jumbo teatowel is a bargain at 6 credits, as this is less than four times the cost of the small teatowel.

You end up 2 credits richer, but with no snow dome.

The Sluggit sold two t-shirts at 4 credits each, so he must have sold four t-shirts at 3 credits each. The Sluggit's total for the day is 20 credits.

SEVEN

DAY EIGHT

NINE

DAY TEN

6	11	4
5	7	**9**
10	3	8
SECRET NUMBER **21**		

10	0	**14**
12	8	4
2	**16**	6
SECRET NUMBER **24**		

8	3	4
1	5	**9**
6	7	2
SECRET NUMBER **15**		

8	6	16
18	10	2
4	14	**12**
SECRET NUMBER **30**		

5	0	7
6	4	2
1	8	**3**
SECRET NUMBER **12**		

3	**4**	10
12	5	0
2	8	7
SECRET NUMBER **17**		

10	8	18
20	12	**4**
6	16	14
SECRET NUMBER **36**		

10	11	**6**
5	9	13
12	7	8
SECRET NUMBER **27**		

10	3	**5**
1	**6**	11
7	**9**	2
SECRET NUMBER **18**		

8	**6**	17
14	**13**	4
9	12	10
SECRET NUMBER **31**		

ELEVEN

DAY TWELVE

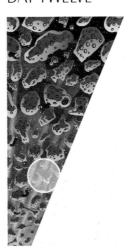

If you are to try every activity and get a smoothie, you will have to buy the 60-credit Multipass and use it on the three most expensive activities. This leaves you with exactly enough to try the remaining activities and buy a smoothie.

SOLUTIONS

DAY THIRTEEN

Your missing luggage was left behind on DAY NINE in the City of Illusion.

The missing crew members were left behind on...

DAY TWO	DAY THREE	DAY FIVE	DAY SEVEN	DAY TWELVE	DAY TWELVE